BASICS for BELIEVING KIDS

A Discipleship Quiet Time Workbook

BETH LIVINGSTON

CREDITS:
Notebook images in every chapter and the praying boy images are designed by Freepik
Calendar and sunshine images are designed by Pixabay

ISBN: 9798637236251

NOTE TO PARENTS

How can we help children who have accepted Christ as Savior grow in their faith? What are the basic things they need to know?

- What does it mean to be a Christian?
- Who is God, Jesus, and the Holy Spirit?
- Why is the Bible important?
- Why pray?
- Why go to church?
- How to tell others about Jesus
- How to have assurance of salvation
- How to be separate from the world
- How to have the character of Christ

Because reading the Bible and praying every day are so important, this is designed as a Quiet Time workbook with daily devotions for twelve weeks. Each week starts with a Phil and Ashley story—a brother and sister who apply these truths.

This can be used by one child alone, by an adult

working one-on-one with a child, as a Bible study for a group of children, or taught as a discipleship class.

It is designed for third-sixth-graders to use independently but can be used by younger children with adult help.

INTRODUCTION

Would you like to know God better? Would you like to know what pleases Him? The Bible tells us how. That's why it is important to read the Bible.

How often should we read the Bible? Every day. Spending time with God every day is called having a Quiet Time. Find a quiet place where no one will bother you, and then read your Bible, pray, and think about God. This will help you know God better.

And this will please God very much.

These lessons start with a story about Phil and Ashley and are followed by Bible verses to read every day and questions to answer. There is also a memory verse to learn each week.

Have a wonderful time getting to know God better!

Beth Livingston

INTRODUCTION

TABLE OF CONTENTS

Am I a Christian?

DAY 1 - Phil and Ashley Story

Phil Denton looked sideways at his best friend Matt. Was Matt listening? Did he understand?

Every day this week Matt had come with him to Vacation Bible School. Today's story was about Jesus dying on the cross, the most important story of all. Why? Because it had changed Phil's life. He wanted it to change Matt's too.

The teacher said, "If Jesus never did anything wrong, why was He nailed to the cross? Because it was God's plan for Jesus to die. You see, no sin is allowed in heaven. But God loved you so much, He wanted you there. So, He made a way for your sin to be forgiven by sending His Son Jesus to shed His blood on the cross.

"Does that mean everyone goes to heaven when they die? No, you must tell Him you want to love and follow Him. How? Tell Him you believe Jesus died and rose again, tell Him you're sorry for your sin, and ask Him to come into your heart and life and take

1

your sin away. Then you will be a child of God, a Christian. Your relationship with God will begin.

"Have you ever done that? If not, you can do it today." The teacher told them to close their eyes. "If you would like to give your life to Jesus, please come up to the front."

Phil squinted at Matt. *Lord, make him go,* Phil prayed.

Matt stood and walked to the front. A teacher took him to another room.

Yes! Thanks, Lord.

Now he wouldn't just be best friends with Matt. They would spend all eternity together.

Talk With God: Talk with God about what you learned from this story.

Memory Verse: (If you would rather memorize this in another Bible translation, that's fine.)

John 3:16 (NIV)- "For God so loved the world that he gave his one and only Son, that whoever believes in him shall not perish but have eternal life."

Explain in your own words what this verse means.

_____

_____

_____

DAY 2

Matt became a Christian that day. So, what is a Christian, anyway? How do you become one?

Read Acts 16:31. (In this verse, being saved means being a Christian.)

What must you do to be saved?

accept Jesus as your LORD and savior read his word and get baptized.

What should you believe about Jesus? Read 1 Corinthians 15:3-4.

1. *died for our sins*
2. *he was burried*
3. *Jesus Rose again the third day*

What else should you believe about Jesus? Read 1 John 4:15.

Jesus is the Son of God

Do you believe these facts about Jesus? *yes*

Talk With God: Thank Jesus, God's Son, for dying on the cross for your sins and rising again.

3

Review your memory verse:

Memory Verse: John 3:16 (NIV)- "For God so loved the world that he gave his one and only Son, that whoever believes in him shall not perish but have eternal life."

DAY 3

You can't do anything to get to heaven on your own. Doing all your chores, being nice to your brother and sister, or obeying your parents will not get you into heaven. You can't be good enough, no matter how hard you try. Why? Because of the sin in you. You must get rid of that sin.

Read Ephesians 2:8-9.

How are we saved?

by grace you are saved.

Grace is God giving you a gift you don't deserve. You don't deserve to go to heaven, but because God loved you and wanted a relationship with you, He sent Jesus to die on the cross to take the punishment for your sin.

Name some ways people try to earn their way to heaven:

going to church, reading the bible, helping people.

None of these ways work. You cannot get to heaven by doing good things, only by believing in Jesus. Jesus did it all.

Talk With God: Thank Jesus for making a way to heaven. Thank Him that you can have a relationship with Him.

Memory Verse: John 3:16 (NIV)- "For God so loved the world that he gave his one and only Son, that whoever believes in him shall not perish but have eternal life."

DAY 4

It is possible to believe that Jesus is the Son of God, that He died on the cross for your sins and rose again three days later, and still not be a Christian. Really?

Read James 2:19 (TLB) - "Are there still some among you who hold that 'only believing' is enough? Believing in one God? Well, remember that the demons believe this too—so strongly that they tremble in terror!"

Even the __devils__ believe in God, and they certainly are not Christians. Demons are evil beings who work for Satan.

Read Romans 10:9.

To be saved, you have to believe with all your __heart__.

What do you think that means?

_____

_____

_____

_____

Do you believe in Jesus with all your heart? __yes__

Talk With God: Tell Jesus what you believe about Him.

Memory Verse: John 3:16 (NIV)- "For God so loved the world that he gave his one and only Son, that whoever believes in him shall not perish but have eternal life."

DAY 5

Have you ever done something wrong and felt really bad about it? Being a Christian is being sorry for your sin and turning away from sin.

Read Acts 20:21(NIV) -"I have declared to both Jews and Greeks that they must turn to God in *repentance* and have faith in our Lord Jesus."

Which word in this verse means turning away from sin? repentance

Repentance is more than being sorry for your sin. It is feeling so bad that you don't ever want to do it again.

Read 1 John 1:9.

What happens when you tell Jesus you are sorry for your sin?

Jesus for your sins

Have you ever told God you are sorry for your sin?

yes

Talk With God: Think of something you've done wrong. Ask God to forgive you and really mean it.

Memory Verse: John 3:16 (NIV)- "For God so loved the world that he gave his one and only Son, that whoever believes in him shall not perish but have eternal life."

DAY 6

Believing also includes accepting or receiving Him.
Read John 1:12 (NLT) -"But to all who believed Him and accepted Him, He gave the right to become children of God."

To accept Christ means asking Him to come into your life. You are sorry for your sin. You give yourself to Jesus and want to follow Him all the days of your life. This makes you a Christian.

Have you asked Jesus to come into your life and forgive your sins? If so, when?

_____

_____

_____

_____

If you have never done this, you can do it right now. Pray something like this:

"Dear God, I believe Jesus died on the cross for my sin and rose again. I am sorry for my sin. Please come into my life and take my sin away. Help me to live for you. In Jesus' name, Amen."

Talk With God: Thank God that you are part of His family.

Memory Verse: John 3:16 (NIV)- "For God so loved the world that he gave his one and only Son, that whoever believes in him shall not perish but have eternal life."

DAY 7

So, what does it mean to be a Christian? Look over your answers from this week.

- You believe that Jesus _____, was buried, and __rose__ again.
- You have told Jesus you are sorry for your __Sins__.
- You have asked Jesus to come into your __heart__.

Are you a Christian? Write down when and where and how old you were when you prayed for Jesus to come into your life.

__I was 13 when I asked Jesus__
__to come in my life, then I got__
__baptized.__

Talk With God: Spend some time picturing Jesus dying on the cross for you. He loves you so much that He would have died even if you were the only person alive.

Memory Verse: John 3:16 (NIV)- "For God so loved the world that he gave his one and only Son, that __died / on the cross__
__for our sins.__

whoever believes in him shall not perish but have eternal life."

Say this verse to someone from memory. Have them initial here when you've done it. _____

What Happened When I Became a Christian?

Day 1- Phil and Ashley Story

Phil's favorite part of Vacation Bible School was game time. Today they played dodge ball.

"Watch out!" Phil yelled as a ball hurtled toward Matt.

Matt didn't see the ball coming. Whomp! It hit him in the nose. Hard.

Matt howled. He fell, his hands over his nose.

The teacher blew his whistle. "Freeze," he shouted as he ran over to Matt. All the kids stopped where they were.

He knelt down and examined Matt's nose. Matt was trying not to cry.

"It's not broken," the teacher said. "Kelsey, run to the nurse for an ice pack. Matt, why don't you sit under the tree for the rest of the game? I'm so sorry that happened." As he stood, he shouted to the others, "No throwing above the neck. Understand?"

Phil sat by Matt as the game continued. "How bad does it hurt?"

"Bad." Matt clenched his teeth. "If I find out who threw that ball, I'll kill him." He added some swear words.

Phil hoped nobody had heard. Christians weren't supposed to swear. Christians weren't supposed to show such anger. But maybe Matt didn't know. After all, he had been a Christian for less than an hour.

"Matt, when you went forward in Bible class today, what did you do?"

"I asked Jesus into my heart."

"Where is Jesus now?"

"In heaven."

"Is He anywhere else?"

Matt paused. "In my heart?"

Phil smiled. "Yes. How do you know He's is your heart? Can you feel Him?"

Matt shook his head.

"It's not Jesus' big body that squeezes into your heart, but the Bible says the Holy Spirit comes to live in you, and He will never leave you. Even when you're a grandpa, Jesus will still be in your heart."

"Cool."

"Since God is living in you and you want to live for Him, do you think you should act any differently?"

Matt looked thoughtful "I guess so."

"The Bible tells us we are born again. We are like new creatures. We shouldn't do the sinful things we did before. Instead, we should be like Jesus."

"I could never be that good."

"Me, either, but we have the Holy Spirit in us to help."

After the game was over, the teacher walked up to Matt with another boy. "Sam has something to tell you."

"I'm sorry I threw the ball at your head," Sam said. "I didn't mean to."

Phil held his breath. Would Matt punch him? Yell at him?

"That's okay," Matt said.

Phil smiled. The Holy Spirit was working in Matt already.

Talk With God: Talk with God about what you learned from this story.

Memory Verse: 2 Corinthians 5:17 (NKJV)- "Therefore, if anyone is in Christ, he is a new creation; old things have passed away; behold, all things have become new."

Explain in your own words what this verse means. If you need help, look back at what Phil said in the story about being a new creature.

_____

_____

_____

DAY 2

Read John 1:12.
When you received or accepted Christ as your Savior, you became a __child__ of God.

You are part of God's family forever and ever. How does that make you feel?

_____happy__ good_____

_____

_____

_____

Talk With God: God is your Father and loves you so much. Tell Him how much you love Him.

Memory Verse: 2 Corinthians 5:17 (NKJV)- "Therefore, if anyone is in Christ, he is a new creation; old things have passed away; behold, all things have become new."

DAY 3

Read John 3:3.

    You can't go to heaven unless you are _____.

This doesn't mean you go back inside your mother. You are too big for that. No, this birth is a spiritual birth.

Read 1 Corinthians 6:19.

When you became a Christian, who came to live within you? _Jesus_

Can you feel the Holy Spirit inside you? Probably not. But we know He is there because the Bible says so.

Who is the Holy Spirit? He is God. There is one God, but He exists in three Persons called the Trinity— The Father, the Son (Jesus), and the Holy Spirit. This is hard to understand. How can one God be three? Sometimes it is helpful to think of water. It can be water or ice or steam— one thing but three different forms. Although we cannot fully understand how God can be three different Persons, we know it is true, and we believe it, because that is what the Bible says.

Being born again is becoming like a new person because you have the Holy Spirit living in you.

Like Matt, you may not be able to feel the Holy Spirit in you. How, then, do you know the Holy Spirit is in you? (If you need help, look at what Phil said in the story.)

_____

_____

_____

_____

Talk With God: Thank God for sending the Holy Spirit to live in you.

Memory Verse: 2 Corinthians 5:17 (NKJV)- "Therefore, if anyone is in Christ, he is a new creation; old things have passed away; behold, all things have become new."

DAY 4

Read 2 Corinthians 5:17. (Or if you can say it from memory, that's even better.)

When you asked Jesus into your heart, what did you become? **A Christian**

In the story, how did Matt show he was a new person?

_____

_____

_____

_____

Think of something you used to think or do that you don't want to anymore since you have Jesus living in you.

_____ *Sinning* _____

_____

_____

_____

Talk With God: Ask Jesus to help you be more like Him.

Memory Verse: 2 Corinthians 5:17 (NKJV)- "Therefore, if anyone is in Christ, he is a new creation; old things have passed away; behold, all things have become new."

DAY 5

Read John 5:24 (HCSB)- "I assure you: Anyone who hears My word and believes Him who sent Me has eternal life and will not come under judgment but has passed from death to life."

When you believe in Jesus, what do you have?

_____

When you die, you will live with Jesus for how long? _eternal_____

Think about living with God forever and ever and ever...with no end ever. Doesn't that blow your mind?

John 5:24 says that you will not be judged for your sins if you believe in Jesus. But those who don't believe in Jesus will have to pay for their sins. What is the penalty (wages) of sin? Read Romans 6:23. _____

This death is separation from God in hell. Hell is an awful place burning with fire where Satan and his demons live. Hell is also eternal. Once you are there, you can never leave. But if you've asked Jesus into your heart, you don't have to worry about hell. You will be safe with God forever.

Talk With God: Praise God that you are safe with Him forever. Thank Him for His love for you.

Memory Verse: 2 Corinthians 5:17 (NKJV)- "Therefore, if anyone is in Christ, he is a new creation; old things have passed away; behold, all things have become new."

DAY 6

When you become a Christian, your sins are forgiven and forgotten by God, paid for on the cross by Jesus.

Read Psalm 103:12 (TLB) - "He has removed our sins as far away from us as the east is from the west."

What happened to our sins?

_____our sins went away?_____

_____

_____

_____

How far is the east from the west? No one can measure it, for the east and west never meet in one point. So, our sins are removed very far away– so far, in fact, that God forgets all about them.

Read Jeremiah 31:34 (NIV)- "...For I will forgive their wickedness and will remember their sins no more."

Underline the part of the verse that tells about God forgetting our sins.

Talk With God: Ask God to show you a sin you need to ask forgiveness for. Tell Him how sorry you are. Thank Jesus for taking away your sin and forgetting all about it.

Memory Verse: 2 Corinthians 5:17 (NKJV)- "Therefore, if anyone is in Christ, he is a new creation; old things have passed away; behold, all things have become new."

DAY 7

L ook back over this week and fill in the blanks. What happened when I became a Christian?

- I became a __Child__ of God.
- The Holy __Spirit__ came to live in me.
- I became a new __person__
- I have __eternal__ life, and I won't go to hell.
- My sins are __forgiven__

Talk With God: Thank Jesus for His love and for the many things He has done for you.

Memory Verse: 2 Corinthians 5:17 (NKJV)- "Therefore, if anyone is in Christ, he is a new creation; old things have passed away; behold, all things have become new."

Say this verse to someone from memory. Have them initial here when you've done it. __S__

See if you can say the memory verse from Week One without looking.

Memory Verse: John 3:16 (NIV)- "For God so loved the world that he gave his one and only Son, that whoever believes in him shall not perish but have eternal life."

Who Is God?

Day 1-Phil and Ashley Story

This would be the best surprise ever.

Ashley had never baked a cake for Mom's birthday. Kelly's mom said she could use her kitchen.

"We did it." Ashley and Kelly grinned at each other as they looked at the lopsided cake.

"It needs candles," Kelly said. "How old is your mom?"

"I don't know," Ashley said. "I'll ask her tonight."

That night when Ashley walked in with the cake, Mom's hands covered her cheeks.

"Happy Birthday!" Ashley said.

"What a wonderful surprise!"

Ashley's smile reached from ear to ear. "I didn't know how many candles to put on. How old are you, Mom?"

"Thirty-nine."

"I didn't know you were that old. You're ancient—almost as old as God."

"Thanks a lot, Ashley." She did not look happy. "But you're wrong. I am not almost as old as God, for

God doesn't have an age."

Ashley frowned. "Everyone has an age."

"Not God. He is eternal. He has no beginning and no end. He always has been."

"But that's impossible. Everyone has to be born sometime."

"God isn't like everyone else. He does not have a mother and father. He has always been alive. We can't fully understand it, but we know it is true because the Bible tells us. Not only is He eternal, but He is holy and powerful and wise and loving and so much more. God is amazing. Ashley, you really should get to know God better."

Ashley nodded thoughtfully. She should.

Talk With God: Talk with God about what you learned from this story.

Memory Verse: I Chronicles 29:11(NIV)- "Yours, O Lord, is the greatness and the power and the glory and the majesty and the splendor, for everything in heaven and earth is yours."

Explain in your own words what this verse means.

The LoRD is our motoVation.

_____

_____

_____

DAY 2- GOD IS ETERNAL

Ashley didn't understand how God had always been alive.

Read Psalm 90:2(TLB)- "Before the mountains were created, before the earth was formed, you are God without beginning or end."

God was around before the _____ or the _____

How is that possible?

_____

_____

_____

_____

Think about God having no beginning or end. It blows your mind, doesn't it?

Talk With God: Tell God you do not understand how He cannot have a beginning or end, but tell Him you believe it.

Memory Verse: 1 Chronicles 29:11(NIV)- "Yours, O Lord, is the greatness and the power and the glory and the majesty and the splendor, for everything in heaven and earth is yours."

DAY 3- GOD IS HOLY

Read 1 Samuel 2:2. Only one is holy. Who?
_____

What is holiness? It means:
1. God is set apart. He is bigger and greater than anything.
2. God is perfect. He has no sin. He can do no evil or wrong.

Read 1 Peter 1:15-16.
What does God want you to be? _____

How can you be holy? Only God is holy. Only God never sins. Why should you even try? Because God wants you to be like Him. He will help you become more like Him and be set apart from the world.

Give an example of how you could be holy.
be helpfull, treat others like you
wanted treated.
_____

_____

Although you will never be perfectly holy in this life, little by little, God can help you be more like him.

Read Philippians 2:13 (NIV)- "For God is working in you, giving you the desire and the power to do what pleases him."

Think back to a year ago. Are you more like Jesus now than you were then? That is the goal.

Talk With God: Ask God to help you become more holy like Him.

Memory Verse: 1 Chronicles 29:11(NIV)- "Yours, O Lord, is the greatness and the power and the glory and the majesty and the splendor, for everything in ⟍ heaven and earth is yours."

DAY 4- GOD IS POWERFUL

Read Jeremiah 32:17.
Because the Lord God is so powerful, what did He make?

God made the heaven and the earth

What is too hard for Him to do? _____

Ready to learn a big word? Omnipotent. That means God is all-powerful. He can do anything, and He never gets tired. There is no one like God.

God is powerful enough to handle all of your problems.

Name a problem you need God's help with right now.

a case I hope my dad gets me back.

Look at this week's memory verse and underline what else you learn about God:

1 Chronicles 29:11(NIV)- "Yours, O Lord, is the greatness and the power and the glory and the majesty and the splendor, for everything in heaven and earth is yours."

Talk With God: Thank God for being so powerful. Ask Him to help you with your problems.

Memory Verse: 1 Chronicles 29:11(NIV)- "Yours, O Lord, is the greatness and the power and the glory and the majesty and the splendor, for everything in heaven and earth is yours."

DAY 5- GOD IS ALL-KNOWING

A nother way to say this is that God is omniscient. Read Psalm 139:1-4. Make a list of what God knows about you.

everything I do in my life.

Read Psalm 147:4. God knows everything. What does God know about the stars?

He tells the number of the stars
he even calls the stars by
their names.

Read Luke 12:7. He even knows

But even the very hairs of your head
are all numbered.

Talk With God: God even knows what you think. Ask God to forgive you for any wrong thoughts you had today.

Memory Verse: 1 Chronicles 29:11(NIV)- "Yours, O Lord, is the greatness and the power and the glory and the majesty and the splendor, for everything in heaven and earth is yours."

DAY 6- GOD IS EVERYWHERE

Read **Jeremiah 23:24 (NCV)**- "No one can hide where I cannot see him," says the Lord. "I fill all of heaven and earth," says the Lord.

Why can't you hide from God?

God is with us everyday

_____

_____

_____

Omnipresent means that God is everywhere at the same time. He can be with you here at the same time He is with a child in China.

Read Proverbs 15:3. God is watching you all the time. What does He see? _____

Read Isaiah 41:10. Who is always with you?

_____

What does He promise to do for you?

give you help

_____

_____

_____

Talk With God: Thank God for being with you always and giving you help and strength.

Memory Verse: 1 Chronicles 29:11(NIV)- "Yours, O Lord, is the greatness and the power and the glory and the majesty and the splendor, for everything in heaven and earth is yours."

DAY 7- GOD IS SOVEREIGN

When we say God is sovereign, it means God controls all things. Nothing happens to you without God's permission.

Job talks to God in Job 42:2(TLB)- "I know that you can do anything and that no one can stop you."

Who can stop God's plan for your life? nobody.

Read Romans 8:28. If you are God's child, what does God promise?

_____

_____

_____

_____

Because God is sovereign, I can trust Him to do what's best for me. Next time you are worried about something, trust God to work everything out.

From what you learned this week, make a list of who God is.

_____

_____

_____

_____

God is awesome, isn't He? And God is much more than this. Keep your eyes open when you read the Bible for things to add.

Talk With God: Thank God for the many ways He is awesome.

Memory Verse: 1 Chronicles 29:11(NIV)- "Yours, O Lord, is the greatness and the power and the glory and the majesty and the splendor, for everything in heaven and earth is yours."

Say this verse to someone by memory. Have them initial here when you've done it. _____

See if you can say the memory verses from Weeks One and Two without looking.

Week 1- John 3:16 (NIV)- "For God so loved the world that he gave his one and only Son, that whoever believes in him shall not perish but have eternal life."

Week 2: 2 Corinthians 5:17 (NKJV)- "Therefore, if anyone is in Christ, he is a new creation; old things have passed away; behold, all things have become new."

Who Is Jesus?

Day 1- Phil and Ashley Story

Phil took one look at the garage sale and returned to the car. It was all girl stuff.

When Mom and Ashley were done shopping, Ashley carried out a large box.

"What did you buy?" he asked.

"A nativity set."

"It's not Christmas. What do you need a Mary and Joseph and baby Jesus for?"

Ashley stuck her nose in the air. "I want to play with it."

"Let her be," Mom said as they drove home.

On the coffee table, Ashley set up Mary, Joseph, Jesus in the manger, shepherds, sheep, donkeys, three wise men, and angels.

As Phil played a video game, Ashley said, "Here I come. I'm Jesus, the Son of God, to save the world." She swooped Jesus down from the sky, landing him in

41

the stable.

"What are you doing, Ashley?" he asked.

"Playing."

"You can't make up things about Jesus. He didn't come to earth like that. He was born as a baby."

"I know."

"So, don't treat Jesus like an action figure. He is holy. He is God's Son. Show Him some honor and respect."

Ashley pouted. "All right... Hmmm...I wonder why He wanted to be a baby."

"He had to be born into our world so He could grow up to die on the cross for our sins."

"But why did He do it that way? Why not just zap our sins away?"

"Because unless blood is shed, sins cannot be forgiven. And unless He became a man, He wouldn't have blood, and He couldn't die."

"Poor baby." Ashley stroked the baby Jesus. "Do you know you'll have to die?"

"He already knew that, Ashley. That's why He came."

"But it's so sad."

"He *wanted* to do it because He loves us so much."

She cuddled the baby in her hand. "Thank You, Jesus."

Phil smiled. She finally got it right.

Talk With God: Talk with God about what you learned from this story.

Memory Verse: Hebrews 9:22 (NIV)- "...without the shedding of blood there is no forgiveness."

Explain in your own words what this verse means.

_____

_____

_____

_____

DAY 2- JESUS IS GOD'S SON

Read Matthew 3:16, 17.
What did God say about Jesus on the day he was baptized?

_____

_____

_____

_____

Read John 3:16. What is Jesus called? _____

Why did God send Jesus into the world?

to forgiv _____

_____

_____

_____

Talk With God: Thank God for loving you so much that He sent His only Son to die for you.

Memory Verse: Hebrews 9:22 (NIV)- "...without the shedding of blood there is no forgiveness."

DAY 3- WHERE DID JESUS COME FROM?

Read John 6:38. Jesus is talking in this verse. Where did Jesus live before he was born on earth?

_____

Who was the one who sent Jesus? _____

This verse also tells why Jesus came. Write the answer here. _____

What was God's will for Jesus? Read John 6:40.

_____

_____

_____

_____

Talk With God: Thank Jesus for being willing to do His Father's will and die on the cross. Tell God you are willing to do what He wants you to do.

Memory Verse: Hebrews 9:22 (NIV)- "...without the shedding of blood there is no forgiveness."

DAY 4- JESUS WAS ALSO MAN

Phil told Ashley that Jesus had to become a man. Read the following verses. How was Jesus like us?

Matthew 4:2- He was _____

John 4:6- He was _____

John 19:28- He was _____

Jesus was like man in every way except for one.

Read 1 Peter 2: 21-22. What was the one way Jesus was different?

_____

_____

_____

_____

Read Hebrews 2:14 (TLB)- "Since we, God's children, are human beings—made of flesh and blood—he became flesh and blood too by being born in human form; for only as a human being could he die and in dying break the power of the devil who had the power of death."

Why did Jesus need to become a man?

1. Only a man could make God known to mankind.

2. Only a man could die.

Talk With God: Thank Jesus for humbling Himself to become a man. Thank Him for dying for you.

Memory Verse: Hebrews 9:22 (NIV)- "...without the shedding of blood there is no forgiveness."

DAY 5- WHY DID JESUS COME TO EARTH?

Read Ephesians 1:5 (TLB)- "His unchanging plan has always been to adopt us into his own family by sending Jesus Christ to die for us. And he did this because he wanted to!"

What was God's plan for Jesus?

_____

_____

_____

_____

Did Jesus want to do it?

_____

_____

_____

_____

Why did Jesus have to die? In the Old Testament, people had to bring a perfect lamb without spot or blemish to the priests in the tabernacle as a sacrifice to cover their sins. Unfortunately, the next time they sinned, another lamb had to die for the new sin.

Because Jesus never sinned, He was without spot or blemish. He was like a perfect lamb, shedding His blood to take away our sin.

Read John 1:29. What did John call Jesus?

_____

Read Romans 6:10(TLB)- "He died once for all to end sin's power."

What do you think "once for all" means?

_____

_____

_____

_____

When Jesus died on the cross, it covered our past, present, and future sins. No other sacrifice ever had to be offered again.

Answer this question: Why did Jesus come to earth?

_____

_____

_____

_____

Just because Jesus died for the sins of the world, it doesn't mean that everyone's sins are forgiven and everyone goes to Heaven. You must believe Jesus died and rose again, and ask Him to forgive you. Then He will come into your heart, and your sins will be taken away.

Do you believe this? _____

Talk With God: Talk with Jesus about what you believe about His death and resurrection. If you have never asked Jesus into your heart before, you can do it today!

Memory Verse: Hebrews 9:22 (NIV)- "...without the shedding of blood there is no forgiveness."

DAY 6- WHY DID JESUS HAVE TO DIE?

Read Hebrews 9:22 (NIV)- "In fact, the law requires that nearly everything be cleansed with blood, and without the shedding of blood there is no forgiveness."

If Jesus hadn't shed his blood for your sins, there would be no _____

Read John 14:6. What is Jesus the way to?

_____

So, why did Jesus have to die on the cross?

_____

_____

_____

_____

Talk With God: Thank Jesus for making a way for you to go to heaven.

Memory Verse: Hebrews 9:22 (NIV)- "...without the shedding of blood there is no forgiveness."

DAY 7- WHERE IS JESUS NOW?

Read Luke 24:1-7. After Jesus died, what happened to Him?

_____

_____

_____

_____

Jesus did not stay dead. He came alive again. Only God could do that.

Read Romans 8:34. Where is Jesus now?

_____

_____

_____

_____

If you are a Christian, where else is He? Read Galatians 4:6.

_____

_____

_____

_____

Talk With God: Thank Jesus for always being there with you.

Memory Verse: Hebrews 9:22 (NIV)- "...without the shedding of blood there is no forgiveness."

Say this verse to someone by memory. Have them initial here when you've done it. _____

See if you can say the memory verses from Weeks Two and Three without looking.

Week 2: 2 Corinthians 5:17 (NKJV)- "Therefore, if anyone is in Christ, he is a new creation; old things have passed away; behold, all things have become new."

Week 3: 1 Chronicles 29:11(NIV)- "Yours, O Lord, is the greatness and the power and the glory and the majesty and the splendor, for everything in heaven and earth is yours."

Who is the Holy Spirit?

Day 1- Phil and Ashley Story

Everything always tasted better cooked over a campfire.

As Phil gobbled his scrambled eggs and bacon, the boy in the next campsite watched him. The boy only had cold cereal for breakfast. He didn't look happy eating with his grandparents.

As they washed their dishes, the boy still stared at them. Phil felt uncomfortable.

"Gather around for devotions," Dad said. After he read a Bible passage, they prayed together. Phil felt even more uncomfortable with the boy watching.

"Who wants to go for a bike ride?" Dad asked.

"I do," Phil and Ashley said.

As they swung onto their bikes, the boy hopped on his. When they pedaled onto the campground road, the boy was right beside them.

Phil wished he would go away. He was tired of

being watched.

"Hi," Dad said. "What's your name?"

"Brody."

"Want to join us?"

"Sure."

Brody was like a shadow. He went to the beach with them. He went on their hike in the woods. At the snack shack, Dad bought him candy too. At least Dad didn't invite him to lunch. But Brody watched their every bite from his campsite.

Phil was sick of it. He wanted time alone. Brody was ruining their weekend.

When Brody's grandma asked him to wash out a pan at the pump, Phil grabbed Ashley's arm. "Quick! Let's get out of here."

Brody didn't see them disappearing into the woods.

When they returned, Brody sat on a stump, drawing circles in the dirt with a stick. He looked bored.

Go talk to him, a voice in Phil's head said. He knew who it was. The Holy Spirit.

He didn't want to.

Go talk to him. Tell him about Jesus.

How could he tell him about Jesus when he had been so mean? Suddenly he felt ashamed of how he had acted.

He walked over to Brody's campsite. "Hey, Brody, want to go fishing with me?"

Brody's face lit up. "Yeah!"

Maybe he would have a chance to tell him about Jesus after all.

Talk With God: Talk with God about what you learned from this story.

Memory Verse: Galatians 5:22-23(NIV)- "But the fruit of the Spirit is love, joy, peace, patience, kindness, goodness, faithfulness, gentleness, and self-control..."

Explain in your own words what this verse means.

_____

_____

_____

_____

DAY 2- WHO IS THE HOLY SPIRIT?

There is one God, but He exists in three Persons called the Trinity—The Father, the Son (Jesus), and the Holy Spirit. This doctrine is hard to understand. How can one God be three? Sometimes it is helpful to think of an egg. It has a shell, a white, and a yolk— one thing but three different forms. Although we cannot fully understand how God can be three different Persons, we believe it, because that is what the Bible says.

Read Matthew 28:19. They were to baptize them in the name of

_____

_____

_____

_____

Read Genesis 1:26. Who do you think the us is referring to?

_____

_____

_____

_____

Who is the Holy Spirit? He is God.

Talk With God: Ask God to help you understand how one God can be three different Persons.

Memory Verse: Galatians 5:22-23(NIV)- "But the fruit of the Spirit is love, joy, peace, patience, kindness, goodness, faithfulness, gentleness, and self-control..."

DAY 3- WHAT DOES THE HOLY SPIRIT DO?

Read John 14:26. Find two or three things Jesus said the Holy Spirit would do.

_____

_____

_____

_____

The moment you accept Christ as your Savior, the Holy Spirit comes to live within you. What does He do?

1. He helps you understand the Bible.
2. He makes you feel guilty when you do something wrong.
3. He helps you obey God.
4. He guides you and helps you know what to do.
5. He helps you be more like Jesus.
6. He helps you pray when you don't know what to say.

Put an X by the ones the Holy Spirit did for Phil in the story.

Circle the ones you have seen the Holy Spirit do for you.

Talk With God: Ask God to help you understand the Bible as you read it.

Memory Verse: Galatians 5:22-23(NIV)- "But the fruit of the Spirit is love, joy, peace, patience, kindness, goodness, faithfulness, gentleness, and self-control..."

DAY 4- HOW DO YOU KNOW THE HOLY SPIRIT IS IN YOU?

When the Holy Spirit lives in you, He produces nine different character traits in your life. This is called the Fruit of the Spirit. Read Galatians 5:22-23 (or say it from memory) and list the nine fruits:

1. _____
2. _____
3. _____
4. _____
5. _____
6. _____
7. _____
8. _____
9. _____

Name one Fruit of the Spirit Phil showed when he asked Brody to go fishing. _____

Give an example of when you experienced one of these things.

_____
_____
_____
_____

Talk With God: Ask God to help the Fruit of the Spirit be seen in you.

Memory Verse: Galatians 5:22-23(NIV)- "But the fruit of the Spirit is love, joy, peace, patience, kindness, goodness, faithfulness, gentleness, and self-control..."

DAY 5- THE HOLY SPIRIT LIVES IN YOU

Read 1 Corinthians 6:19-20 (TLB)- "Haven't you yet learned that your body is the home of the Holy Spirit God gave you, and that he lives within you? Your own body does not belong to you. For God has bought you with a great price. So use every part of your body to give glory back to God, because he owns it."

Where does the Holy Spirit live? _____

Who does your body belong to? _____

How are we to use our bodies?

_____

_____

_____

_____

Can you think of a way that you can honor or give glory back to God?

_____

_____

_____

_____

Talk With God: Ask the Holy Spirit to help you use your life to bring praise to God.

Memory Verse: Galatians 5:22-23(NIV)- "But the fruit of the Spirit is love, joy, peace, patience, kindness, goodness, faithfulness, gentleness, and self-control..."

DAY 6- POWER!

R ead Acts 1:8.
What does the Holy Spirit give you? _____
What is that power to be used for?

_____
_____
_____
_____

It can be scary telling someone else about Jesus, but the Holy Spirit can give you the words to say.

Read Philippians 4:13 (TLB)- "For I can do everything God asks me to with the help of Christ who gives me the strength and power."

What can you do when Christ or the Holy Spirit gives you power?

_____
_____
_____
_____

Talk With God: Thank God for being so powerful and for helping you.

Memory Verse: Galatians 5:22-23 (NIV)- "But the fruit of the Spirit is love, joy, peace, patience, kindness, goodness, faithfulness, gentleness, and self-control..."

DAY 7- CAN I MAKE THE HOLY SPIRIT SAD?

What does the Bible tell you not to do to the Holy Spirit?

Ephesians 4:30 _____

That's what Phil did when he had such a rotten attitude about Brody.

If you are a Christian, the Holy Spirit will never come out of your heart. But when you sin, it grieves the Holy Spirit or makes him sad. It also makes Him sad when you know what the Holy Spirit wants you to do, but you don't do it. Fortunately, Phil did what he knew the Holy Spirit wanted him to do.

If you have grieved the Holy Spirit, what can you do to make Him happy again?

_____

_____

_____

_____

Talk With God: Tell Jesus you are sorry for any and all sin you have done recently.

Memory Verse: Galatians 5:22-23(NIV)- "But the fruit of the Spirit is love, joy, peace, patience, kindness, goodness, faithfulness, gentleness, and self-control..."

Say this verse to someone by memory. Have them initial here when you've done it. _____

See if you can say the memory verses from Weeks Three and Four without looking.

Week 3: 1 Chronicles 29:11(NIV)- "Yours, O Lord, is the greatness and the power and the glory and the majesty and the splendor, for everything in heaven and earth is yours."

Week 4: Hebrews 9:22 (NIV)- "...without the shedding of blood there is no forgiveness."

Why is the Bible So Important?

Day 1- Phil and Ashley Story

When it was Mom's turn to work in the church nursery, Ashley helped. Ashley loved babies.

The cutest of all was chubby Maddie. Ashley played with her until Maddie cried. "What's wrong with her? Did I do something wrong?"

"She's probably hungry. Let me get her bottle." Mom pulled a bottle from her diaper bag. "Would you like to feed her?"

"Yes!"

Mom laid the baby in her lap and handed her the bottle of milk. Now Maddie was screaming.

"Is this all she gets?" Ashley asked. "I don't think milk is enough to fill her up. She's really hungry. Don't we have anything else?"

"No, she's not old enough for anything else. All she needs is milk to help her grow."

Ashley stuck the bottle in her mouth. Maddie sucked and quieted.

"I don't get it. If all I had was milk, I wouldn't grow much."

"That's because you're older, and your body can handle meats and vegetables. It reminds me of when you ask Jesus into your heart. You are a baby Christian. All you can handle is the milk of the Word of God, or the easiest things."

Ashley wrinkled her nose. "'I don't get it. I can't drink milk from the Bible."

"No, but you can *read* the Bible. As you read it, the Holy Spirit helps you understand it. And the more you understand and obey, the more you will be like Christ. That's growing. Then you'll be ready to understand harder things, or the meat of the Word."

"Am *I* ready for meat yet?" Ashley asked.

Mom smiled. "Almost. You're still a baby Christian. Keep reading your Bible every day. Keep growing."

Ashley tipped the bottle so Maddie could drink every last drop. Was she as hungry to read her Bible as Maddie was for her milk?

Not really. Maybe she did have more growing to do.

Talk With God: Talk with God about what you learned from this story.

Memory Verse: 1 Peter 2:2(NKJV)- "As newborn babes, desire the pure milk of the word that you may grow thereby."

Explain in your own words what this verse means. If you need help, look back at what Mom said in the story.

_____

_____

_____

_____

DAY 2

If you have recently received Christ as your Savior, 1 Peter 2:2 tells what you are.

1 Peter 2:2(NKJV)- "As newborn babes, desire the pure milk of the word that you may grow thereby."

What does this verse say you are like? a child of God

In the story, Mom called Ashley a baby Christian. This is not a bad thing. It just means she was a new Christian. Ashley still has a lot to learn about Jesus, and so do you. This workbook will help you learn the basics about being a Christian. It will help you grow.

As a newborn baby in Christ, it is important to grow as fast as possible. What helps you grow according to 1 Peter 2:2

_____

_____

_____

_____

Just as your body needs food to be strong, so you need the Bible, the Word of God, to feed you and help you grow spiritually. Why, then, is it important to read the Bible every day?

_____

_____

_____

_____

Do you read the Bible every day? _____

Talk With God: Ask the Holy Spirit to help you understand what you read in the Bible and to be faithful to read it every day.

Memory Verse: 1 Peter 2:2(NKJV)- "As newborn babes, desire the pure milk of the word that you may grow thereby."

DAY 3

Read 2 Timothy 3:16-17 (TLB)- "The whole Bible was given to us by inspiration from God and is useful to teach us what is true and to make us realize what is wrong in our lives; it straightens us out and helps us do what is right."

When it says the Bible was inspired by God, it means that the Holy Spirit guided men to write down what God wanted. Everything in the Bible is true because it is from God.

What does 2 Timothy 3:16-17 say the Bible is useful for?

1. _____
2. _____
3. _____
4. _____

When has the Bible helped you? What has the Bible shown you was wrong?

_____
_____
_____
_____

Talk With God: Ask God to help you do right and to show you if you have done anything else wrong.

Memory Verse: 1 Peter 2:2(NKJV)- "As newborn babes, desire the pure milk of the word that you may grow thereby."

DAY 4

Read Psalm 119:11.
Why do we need to read God's Word?

_____

_____

_____

_____

    Memorizing verses from the Bible is a good way to hide God's Word in your heart. That's why it's so important to learn these memory verses each week.
    Read Psalm 119:105. Write it in your own words what you think this means.

_____

_____

_____

_____

Talk With God: Ask God to use His Word to show you how to love Him and live for Him.

Memory Verse: 1 Peter 2:2(NKJV)- "As newborn babes, desire the pure milk of the word that you may grow thereby."

DAY 5

R ead Joshua 1:8.
What should we do day and night?

meditate on God's word

To meditate mean to think about. When you read the Bible, it is important to think about what you've read and remember it all through the day. Why does Joshua 1:8 say we should do this?

to do what all is written

If we meditate on God's Word day and night and try our best to obey it, what does God promise?

1. _____

2. _____

Practice meditating on Joshua 1:8 today.

Talk With God: Ask God to help you obey what the Bible says.

Memory Verse: 1 Peter 2:2(NKJV)- "As newborn babes, desire the pure milk of the word that you may grow thereby."

DAY 6

Read Hebrews 4:12(NIV)- "For the word of God is living and active. Sharper than any two-edged sword, it penetrates even to dividing soul and spirit, joints and marrow; it judges the thoughts and attitudes of the heart."

How can the Bible be living? Isn't it only a book? No, it isn't. When you read the Bible, the Holy Spirit helps you understand it and speaks to your heart. The Holy Spirit makes it come alive for you, and it changes your heart so you will be more like Jesus.

How is the Bible like a sword?

it Can protect you

it Can help you

_____

_____

_____

Talk With God: Ask God to show you if any of your thoughts do not please Him and ask Him to change your heart to be more like His.

Memory Verse: 1 Peter 2:2(NKJV)- "As newborn babes, desire the pure milk of the word that you may grow thereby."

DAY 7

Look over this week's lessons and in your own words tell why God's Word is important.

_____

_____

_____

_____

Because God's Word is so important, you should read it every day. This is called having a Quiet Time. Find a quiet place where you can be alone with God. What do you do in a Quiet Time?

- Read a few verses in the Bible. Read it as if it were a letter from God just to you.
- Think about what you have read. What does it say about who God is? How does it apply to you?
- Praise and worship God.
- Confess your sins.
- Pray for others and yourself.

Let's practice. Read the first part of Psalm 46:10. (NLT)- "Be still, and know that I am God!"
What does this verse mean?

_____

_____

_____

_____

How can you do what this verse says?

_____

_____

_____

_____

Talk With God: Think of everything you know about God and thank Him for being so great. Tell Jesus you are sorry for your sins. Pray for yourself and others.

Memory Verse: 1 Peter 2:2(NKJV)- "As newborn babes, desire the pure milk of the word that you may grow thereby."

Say this verse to someone by memory. Have them initial here when you've done it. _____

See if you can say the memory verses from Weeks Four and Five without looking.

Week 4: Hebrews 9:22 (NIV)- "...without the shedding of blood there is no forgiveness."

Week 5: Galatians 5:22-23(NIV)- "But the fruit of the Spirit is love, joy, peace, patience, kindness, goodness, faithfulness, gentleness, and self-control..."

WEEK 7

Why Pray?

Day 1- Phil and Ashley Story

Dear Lord, You know how much I want to play football this summer, Phil prayed. *Please help me make the team. In Jesus' name, Amen.*

Phil closed his Bible and slid off the bed. He had just read in Matthew 21:22 that if he believed, he would receive whatever he asked God for. Now he would see if it was true.

He found Dad in his recliner in the family room. "Dad, I would like to play flag football this summer."

Dad looked up. "Oh, really? Since when?"

"Since Matt is going to sign up. There are only a few spots left."

"When does it meet? How much does it cost?"

With a few clicks, Dad brought up the website. He frowned as he scrolled down. "Phil, the games are on Sunday mornings."

"Really?" Phil didn't know that.

"I'm sorry, but no. Church is more important than football."

"But..." Phil knew Dad was right, but he really wanted to play. "Dad, God promised to give me whatever I prayed for."

"If it's His will."

"What does that mean?"

"When you pray for something God wants for you, He will give it to you. But if you are praying for something that does not honor God or is not good for you, then God may not answer your prayer the way you want. God always does what is best for you."

Playing football on Sunday morning when he should be worshipping in church would definitely not bring honor to God. Dad was right, but he was still disappointed.

"Then why pray about anything?" Phil asked.

"Because God tells us to. Prayer makes us feel closer to God, and prayer unleashes the power of God."

Phil nodded. He did feel close to God when he prayed.

"Hey, Phil, look at this." Dad scrolled down on the website. "Another team meets on Tuesday nights. We could do that one."

Phil grinned. God had answered his prayer after all—not how he'd asked but better.

Talk With God: Talk with God about what you learned from this story.

Memory Verse: Matthew 21:22 (NIV)- "And all things, whatever you ask in prayer, believing, you will receive."

Explain in your own words what this verse means.

_____

_____

_____

_____

DAY 2

Prayer is talking with God. You don't have close your eyes, bow your head, or talk out loud. You can just *think* the words, and God will hear you.

Read 1 Thessalonians 5:17.

How often should you pray? Before every meal? Before bedtime? What does this verse say?

_____

_____

_____

_____

How is that possible? You can't pray every minute. No, but God wants you to talk to Him often throughout the day.

Talk With God: Today try to talk to God all through the day. Thank Him for something. Tell Him you love Him. Tell Him about something bothering you. Ask Him to show you what to do.

At the end of the day, if you did that, put an X here._____

Memory Verse: Matthew 21:22 (NIV)- "And all things, whatever you ask in prayer, believing, you will receive."

DAY 3

Although Jesus was God and was constantly connected to God the Father, He still prayed. Read Mark 1:35. When did He pray?

_____

_____

_____

_____

How long did He pray in Luke 6:12?

_____

If Jesus needed to pray, so do we!

Talk With God: You don't have to pray all night like Jesus did, but today try to spend at least five minutes talking with God.

Memory Verse: Matthew 21:22 (NIV)- "And all things, whatever you ask in prayer, believing, you will receive."

DAY 4

Phil thought he would receive whatever he prayed for. But God wants you to do certain things first. Find out what they are in the following verses.

Matthew 7:7,8

_____

_____

_____

_____

Matthew 21:22

_____

_____

_____

_____

1 John 3:22

_____

_____

_____

_____

1 John 5:14-15

_____

_____

_____

_____

Talk With God: Ask God to help you love, obey, and follow Him.

Memory Verse: Matthew 21:22 (NIV)- "And all things, whatever you ask in prayer, believing, you will receive."

DAY 5

There are three ways God may answer your prayer:
1. Yes
2. No
3. Wait

Read James 4:3 (TLB)- "And even when you do ask you don't get it because your whole aim is wrong— you want only what will give you pleasure."

What can keep you from getting what you ask God for?

_____

_____

_____

_____

You should pray for God's will to be done and not what you want. Why? Because God knows what is best for you.

What else can keep God from hearing your prayer?

Read Psalm 66:18, 19 (TLB)- "He would not have listened if I had not confessed my sins. But He listened! He heard my prayer! He paid attention to it!"

God will not listen to your prayer if

_____

_____

_____

_____

When you sin, ask God to forgive you.

Talk With God: Pray for God's will to be done in your life. Ask God to show you any sinful things you have done or thought yesterday or today. Ask God to forgive you.

Memory Verse: Matthew 21:22 (NIV)- "And all things, whatever you ask in prayer, believing, you will receive."

DAY 6

Prayer made Phil feel closer to God. Why?
  Read James 4:8 (NIV)- "Come near to God and He will come near to you."

  When you come into God's presence in prayer, what does He promise?

_____

_____

_____

_____

  How awesome is that? You will be close to God.

Talk With God: Imagine that Jesus is in the room with you and that you are kneeling at His feet. Feel His closeness.

Memory Verse: Matthew 21:22 (NIV)- "And all things, whatever you ask in prayer, believing, you will receive."

DAY 7

Prayer is not only asking God for things, it is also thanking and praising Him.

Read Psalm 100:4-5. What are some reasons we should praise Him?

1. _____
2. _____
3. _____

Read 1 Thessalonians 5:18. How many things should we thank God for?

_____

_____

_____

_____

What if something bad happens to you? Can you still be thankful? Yes. Read Romans 8:28 and write down why.

_____

_____

_____

_____

Talk With God: Instead of asking God for something today, spend the time thanking Him for who He is and what He has done for you.

Memory Verse: Matthew 21:22 (NIV)- "And all things, whatever you ask in prayer, believing, you will receive."

Say this verse to someone by memory. Have them initial here when you've done it. _____

See if you can say the memory verses from Weeks Five and Six without looking.

Week 5: Galatians 5:22-23(NIV)- "But the fruit of the Spirit is love, joy, peace, patience, kindness, goodness, faithfulness, gentleness, and self-control..."

Week 6: 1 Peter 2:2(NKJV)- "As newborn babes, desire the pure milk of the word that you may grow thereby."

Why Go to Church?

Day 1- Phil and Ashley Story

Ashley stopped at the door of her Sunday school classroom. Only her teacher was at the table.

"Ashley, I'm so glad you're here," Mrs. Ball said.

"Where is everyone?" Ashley asked.

"I guess they're not coming today." Mrs. Ball looked sad.

"Why not?"

"They must have had other things to do."

Ashley remembered that sometimes Keesha went to their lake house on summer weekends. Kelly was on vacation. Didn't Omar join a soccer team? And Colby just didn't show up very often.

It wasn't much fun being the only one.

Later, when Ashley rode home with her parents and Phil, she said, "I was the only one in my class today. It was awful. Maybe I'll stay home next week."

"No, you won't," Dad said. "We always go to

church on Sunday."

"But why? Why go to church?"

"First, the Bible tells us to, and obeying God is always the right choice. Secondly, it's where we hear God's Word preached and learn who God is and how to live for Him."

"But couldn't I watch church on TV?"

"Yes," Mom said, "but it's not the same. There's something really special about worshiping God together with others."

"Plus, it's where our friends are," Phil said.

He was right. She loved seeing her friends.

Now she felt sorry for all her friends who hadn't come today. They had missed out.

Talk With God: Talk to God about what you learned from this story.

Memory Verse: Psalm 122:1(NKJV)- "I was glad when they said to me, 'Let us go into the house of the Lord.'"

Explain in your own words what this verse means.

to hear and listen to God's word.

_____

_____

_____

DAY 2

You have already learned two ways to know Jesus better and grow in your faith—reading your Bible and praying. Another is going to a church that teaches about Jesus.

Read Hebrews 10:25 (TLB)- "Let us not neglect our church meetings, as some people do, but encourage and warn each other, especially now that the day of His coming back again is drawing near."

What does this verse tell us to do?

draw near to God

Do you go to church every week? If not, ask your mom or dad to take you. Find a church with a Sunday school or a kids' club during the week where you can learn more about Jesus.

If your parents will not take you to church, maybe a friend will. If no one will, keep reading your Bible on your own and pray that someday God would provide a way for you to go to church.

Talk With God: Talk with God about why you want to go to church.

Memory Verse: Psalm 122:1(NKJV)- "I was glad when they said to me, 'Let us go into the house of the Lord.'"

DAY 3

Have you ever felt like Ashley— that you just didn't feel like going to church?

Read Psalm 122:1. (This is your memory verse for this week. Can you say it without looking yet?)

What should be your attitude about going to church? _____

How do you think God feels if you grumble about going to church? _____

Check your attitude next Sunday. Make God happy.

Talk With God: Thank God for your pastor and teachers who help you learn more about Jesus.

Memory Verse: Psalm 122:1(NKJV)- "I was glad when they said to me, 'Let us go into the house of the Lord.'"

DAY 4

R ead Psalm 27:4.
What was one thing the writer David wanted?

_____

"The house of the Lord" is talking about being close to God. Name some ways you can draw closer to God in church.

1. _____
2. _____

Talk With God: Picture yourself kneeling at Jesus feet. Talk to Him about how much you love Him.

DAY 5

Read Acts 2:42(NIV)- "They devoted themselves to the apostles' teaching and to the fellowship, to the breaking of bread and to prayer."

This describes the very first churches. They didn't meet in church buildings but in people's homes. They did four things in these early churches. Draw a line to describe what they did.

Teaching

Fellowship

Breaking of bread

Prayer

Talking with God

Spending time with each other

Learning about God

Communion service: Eating bread to symbolize Christ's body and drinking wine or juice to symbolize Christ's blood.

Put an X by the things you do at your church.

Talk With God: Pray for your church. Ask God to bless it. Pray that people would draw closer to Jesus.

Memory Verse: Psalm 122:1(NKJV)- "I was glad when they said to me, 'Let us go into the house of the Lord.'"

DAY 6

Ashley missed not having her friends at church. One of the best things about church is hanging out with your Christian friends. This is called fellowship. Read Acts 2:42 again.

What is fellowship? The dictionary defines it as "being together or sharing similar interests or experiences." List some similar interests or experiences you have with other kids at church:

1. _____
2. _____
3. _____

Talk With God: Ask God to show you how to be a better friend to the kids at church.

Memory Verse: Psalm 122:1(NKJV)- "I was glad when they said to me, 'Let us go into the house of the Lord.'"

DAY 7

Read 2 Corinthians 6:14-15 (HCSB)- "Do not be mismatched with unbelievers. For what partnership is there between righteousness and lawlessness? Or what fellowship does light have with darkness? ...Or what does a believer have in common with an unbeliever?"

Why is it better for your closest friends to be Christian kids?

_____

_____

_____

_____

It is good to have non-Christian friends so you can be a light to show them who Jesus is, but your best friends should be Christians because you have more in common with them.

This is especially true when you are older and choosing someone to marry. If you have Jesus in your heart, you are not to marry someone who is not a Christian. Why? Because the most important thing to you (Jesus) is not important to them. They may pull you away from God. They may do things you would never do, and this will make you unhappy. You will be disobeying God if you marry someone who is not a Christian.

Decide right now that you will never marry or even date someone who is not a Christian.

Talk With God: Talk to God about how He is the most important person in your life. Ask God to help you put Him first.

Memory Verse: Psalm 122:1(NKJV)- "I was glad when they said to me, 'Let us go into the house of the Lord.'"

Say this verse to someone by memory. Have them initial here when you've done it.

See if you can say the memory verses from Weeks Six and Seven without looking.

Week 6: 1 Peter 2:2(NKJV)- "As newborn babes, desire the pure milk of the word that you may grow thereby."

Week 7: Matthew 21:22 (NIV)- "And all things, whatever you ask in prayer, believing, you will receive."

How Do I Tell Others About Jesus?

Day 1- Phil and Ashley Story

"Batter up!"

Phil stepped up to the plate for the neighborhood baseball game. He practiced several swings with his bat. He was ready.

The pitcher threw the ball. Closer and closer it came. THWACK!

It was a solid hit. He took off for first base as the ball flew.

"Go," his teammates yelled.

He ran to second base. "Go," they yelled again.

He ran to third base. "Go!"

Phil slid into home plate before the catcher caught the ball.

A home run! His first ever. They won 7-6.

"Way to go, Phil." His teammates high-fived him.

Phil grinned.

Suddenly a hand snatched the cap off his head. He spun around. It was Darren, a player from the losing team.

Phil reached for his cap. "Hey, give it back."

Instead, Darren threw it to the ground and stomped on it. "That's what I think of you, Mr. Hotshot."

Everyone watched in stunned silence. Phil knew they expected him to fight back. He wanted to, but what kind of example would that be? Instead, he said, "You can keep the hat if you want."

As he walked away, footsteps ran behind him. Pete, a guy on his team, caught up with him. "Why did you do that?" he asked. "Why were you so nice to him? Why didn't you fight back?"

Here was an opportunity to be a light for Jesus. "Jesus wanted me to forgive him, not fight."

Pete frowned. "What does Jesus have to do with it?"

"Everything. I've asked Jesus to come into my life, and I want to please Him in all I do."

Pete's eyebrows lifted. "You're weird, Phil. Nice, but totally different."

Phil grinned. Nice and different?

Score one for Jesus.

Talk With God: Talk with God about what you learned from this story.

Memory Verse: Mark 16:15 (NKJV)- "And He said to them, 'Go into all the world and preach the gospel to every creature.'"

Explain in your own words what this verse means.

tell everyone about jesus

_____

_____

_____

_____

DAY 2

Telling others about Jesus with the hope of them believing and following Jesus is called witnessing or evangelism. God wants you to witness.

Read Mark 16:15. (This is your memory verse for the week.)

What did Jesus tell his disciples to do?

_____

_____

_____

_____

What is the gospel or good news? (See 1 Corinthians 15:3-4.)

_____

_____

_____

_____

Have you ever told anyone about Jesus?

_____

Talk With God: Ask God to give you the courage to tell someone about Jesus this week.

Memory Verse: Mark 16:15 (NKJV)- "And He said to them, 'Go into all the world and preach the gospel to every creature.'"

DAY 3

It can be scary telling people about Jesus, and we can't do it in our own strength.

Read Acts 1:8.

Where do we get the power to witness?

_____

The Holy Spirit will give you the words to say if you depend on Him.

Talk With God: Ask the Holy Spirit to help you not be afraid to tell others about Jesus.

Memory Verse: Mark 16:15 (NKJV)- "And He said to them, 'Go into all the world and preach the gospel to every creature.'"

DAY 4

People may not receive Jesus the first time you tell them. It may take years before they believe.

Read 1 Corinthians 3:6-7(NIV)- "I (Paul) planted the seed, Apollos watered it, but God made it grow. So neither he who plants nor he who waters is anything, but only God, who makes things grow."

The seed is the truth in the Word of God.

In witnessing, what do you think it means to plant the seed?

_____

_____

_____

_____

What do you think it means to water the seed?

_____

_____

_____

_____

You can plant and water by telling someone about Jesus, but who is the one who makes the seed grow?

_____

_____

_____

_____

God wants you to tell people about Jesus. Then He works in their hearts to make them want to accept

Him. You cannot force anyone to believe in Jesus, but you can pray for them.

Write down the name of one person you know who is not a Christian. <u>forge</u>

Talk With God: Pray for that person to accept Jesus as their Savior.

Memory Verse: Mark 16:15 (NKJV)- "And He said to them, 'Go into all the world and preach the gospel to every creature.'"

DAY 5

Why is it important to tell others about Jesus? Read John 3:36.

What are the two types of people in the world?

1. _non christians_
2. _christians_

Which are you? _Christian_

What happens to those who don't believe in Jesus?

They don't have eternal life, and don't hear God's word.

This is very sad. Our loved ones and friends who do not believe in Jesus as their Savior will go to hell when they die. Hell is an awful place burning with fire where Satan and his demons live.

Talk With God: Pray again for the person whose name you wrote down yesterday.

Memory Verse: Mark 16:15 (NKJV)- "And He said to them, 'Go into all the world and preach the gospel to every creature.'"

DAY 6

One of the best ways to share Jesus is to be a friend. When kids see you acting like Jesus as Phil did, they may ask you, "What makes you so nice?" or "What makes you so happy?" or "What makes you different?" That gives you the perfect opening to tell them how you've asked Jesus to come into your heart to take your sin away.

Read Matthew 5:14-16.

What are you supposed to be?

_____

_____

_____

_____

Name some ways you could let your light shine for Jesus:

_____

_____

_____

_____

Talk With God: Ask God to help you be a light to the world so that others will see Jesus in you.

Memory Verse: Mark 16:15 (NKJV)- "And He said to them, 'Go into all the world and preach the gospel to every creature.'"

DAY 7

Read 1 Peter 3:15.
What should we always be ready to do?

_____

_____

_____

_____

If someone asks you about Jesus, would you know what to say? It might be helpful for you to have a tract to share with them. Child Evangelism Fellowship publishes some wonderful tracts: https://cefpress.com/evangelism/tracts-for-children/

Basically, this is what you need to share:

1. God loves you.
John 3:16 (NIV)- "For God so loved the world that he gave his one and only Son, that whoever believes in him shall not perish but have eternal life."

2. But... you were born with a sin problem. Sin separates you from a holy God.
Romans 3:23(HCSB)- "For all have sinned and fall short of the glory of God.

3. The penalty for your sin must be paid.
Romans 6:23(HCSB)- "For the wages of sin is death, but the gift of God is eternal life in Christ Jesus our Lord."

The penalty for sin is being sent to hell when

you die. But God loved you so much, he didn't want you to go there. So, He made a way for you to have your sins forgiven.

4. Jesus Christ died for you.
1 Corinthians 15:3b-4(HCSB)- "That Christ died for our sins according to the Scriptures, that He was buried, that He was raised on the third day according to the Scriptures."

Jesus died on the cross and shed his blood to take the punishment for your sins. Then on the third day, He rose from the dead. Jesus is alive today in Heaven.

5. What must you do to be saved?
Just because Jesus died, doesn't mean everyone goes to Heaven when they die.

Acts 16:31(HCSB)- "Believe on the Lord Jesus, and you will be saved."

You must believe that Jesus died and rose again for you. Tell Him you're sorry for your sin. Ask him to come into your heart and forgive you. Pray something like this:

"Dear Jesus,

Thanks for loving me and dying on the cross for my sin. Please forgive me for the wrong things I've done. Please come into my heart and life and take my sin away. In Jesus' name, Amen."

It would be helpful for you to memorize these verses so you are always ready if someone asks you about Jesus.

Talk With God: Ask God to help you share with others what He did for you.

Memory Verse: Mark 16:15 (NKJV)- "And He said to them, 'Go into all the world and preach the gospel to every creature.'"

Say this verse to someone by memory. Have them initial here when you've done it. _____

See if you can say the memory verses from Weeks Seven and Eight without looking.

Week 7: Matthew 21:22 (NIV)- "And all things, whatever you ask in prayer, believing, you will receive."

Week 8: Psalm 122:1(NKJV)- "I was glad when they said to me, 'Let us go into the house of the Lord.'"

If I Sin Will Jesus Come Out of My Heart?

Day 1- Phil and Ashley Story

She wasn't a girl Ashley wanted to hang out with. Mrs. Stevens stood in the Sunday school classroom with a girl who looked as if she hadn't washed her hair in ages. Her jeans were too short. Her sneakers were ripped.

"Mrs. Ball," Mrs. Stevens said, "I'd like you to meet my new neighbor Katie. This is her first time in Sunday school."

Mrs. Ball smiled. "We're glad you're here, Katie. Have a seat." Katie sat in the empty chair next to Ashley.

Pee-yew. She smelled. Ashley scooted away.

When it was time to move to the next room, she whispered to her best friend Kelly, "Don't sit near her. She stinks."

Ashley and Kelly sat together. When Katie sat next to them, Ashley and Kelly looked at each other, giggled, stood up, and moved to the front row, leaving Katie behind.

Katie did not come the next Sunday. Mrs. Ball said, "I'm disappointed in you, class. Last week we had a guest. She was laughed at and made to feel so unwelcome that she said she wouldn't come again. It's because of you that she may never hear more about Jesus."

Ashley felt terrible. It was all her fault. She was the one who had been so mean.

In the car on the way home, she was worried. She asked Mom and Dad, "If I do something really bad, will Jesus come out of my heart?"

"What did you do now?" Phil grinned.

She stuck out her tongue at him.

"When you ask Jesus to come into your heart, He will never leave you," Mom said. "Ever."

Ashley breathed a sigh of relief.

"But," Dad said, "when you sin, you won't feel as close to Jesus anymore."

That was true. Jesus felt far away now. He was not happy with how she had treated Katie.

"What do I have to do to feel close again?"

"Confess your sin. Tell God you're sorry."

All right, she would. She prayed silently, *Dear Jesus, please forgive me for being so mean to Katie. I am really sorry. Please give me another chance.*

Phil nudged her. "So, what did you do that was so bad?"

"None of your business."

Phil didn't need to know. It was taken care of. God had forgiven her.

But she felt she should do more. That afternoon she called Mrs. Stevens and asked for Katie's address. Then she wrote a note:

Dear Katie,

My name is Ashley Denton. I am the girl who sat next to you in church and was so mean to you. Jesus has shown me how wrong I was. I have asked His forgiveness, and now I ask for yours. I hope you will come back to church. I will save a seat for you. I would like to be your friend.

Sincerely,
Ashley Denton

Katie came back next Sunday, and Ashley was so happy that she never once noticed her smell.

Talk With God: Talk with God about what you learned from this story.

Memory Verse: Hebrews 13:5 (HCSB)- "I will never leave you or forsake you."

Explain in your own words what this verse means.

Jesus will always be with us no matter what.

DAY 2

Although Jesus was not happy with how Ashley had treated Katie, He still loved her and always would.

Read Hebrews 13:5 (HCSB)- "I will never leave you or forsake you."

What does God promise?

_____

_____

_____

_____

Read Isaiah 59:2. What happens when we sin?

but your iniquities have Separated between you and your God, and your Sins have hid his face from you, that he will not hear.

When you sin, Jesus does not come out of your heart, but, like Ashley, you won't feel as close to Him. How can you feel close again? Read 1 John 1:9.

_____

_____

_____

When you ask God to forgive you, what does He promise to do?

_____

_____

_____

_____

Then you will feel close to God again.

Talk With God: Ask God to forgive you for any and all recent sin.

Memory Verse: Hebrews 13:5 (HCSB)- "I will never leave you or forsake you."

DAY 3

Read John 5:24(HCSB)- "I assure you: Anyone who hears My word and believes Him who sent Me has eternal life and will not come under judgment but has passed from death to life."

If you have received Jesus as your personal Savior, what does this verse say you have?

¿ you have eternal life

How long is eternal? _forever_

That means you will always have it. Nothing can take it away. You know you will go to heaven when you die.

Talk With God: Thank God that you will live with Him forever and ever.

Memory Verse: Hebrews 13:5 (HCSB)- "I will never leave you or forsake you."

DAY 4

R ead John 10:28.
    If you have eternal life and are safe in God's
hand, what will never happen?

_____

_____

_____

_____

If it were possible to lose eternal life, then it would
not be eternal. When you are saved, you are saved
forever. You do not hold onto God. He holds onto you.

Talk With God: Thank God for keeping you safe in
His hands.

Memory Verse: Hebrews 13:5 (HCSB)- "I will never
leave you or forsake you."

DAY 5

God guarantees your salvation. Read Romans 8:38-39.

What can separate you from the love of God?

not talking to God or
not having a daily relationship

_____

_____

Jesus will never come out of your heart. How does that make you feel?

happy

_____

_____

_____

Talk With God: Thank God for loving you so much.

Memory Verse: Hebrews 13:5 (HCSB)- "I will never leave you or forsake you."

DAY 6

Read John 3:16 (or say it from memory).
What do you need to do to have eternal life?

For God so loved the world,that he gave his
only begotten son,that whosoever
believes in him should not perish, but
have everlasting

Why did God give His only Son?

to forgive everybody
for their sins

Are you sure you will go to heaven when you
die? I hope

Talk With God: Thank Jesus for loving you and saving you a place in heaven.

Memory Verse: Hebrews 13:5 (HCSB)- "I will never leave you or forsake you."

DAY 7

Read Revelation 21:27.
Who are the only people who will be allowed in heaven?

The people who accepted Jesus.

The Lamb's Book of Life is a book in heaven with the names of people who believe in Jesus as their Savior.

Read Ephesians 1:4. If you are a Christian, when did God choose you?

Your name was written in the Lamb's Book of Life before the world was even created. And your name cannot be erased, so God is saving a place for you in heaven. You can count on it!

Answer this question: If I sin will Jesus come out of my heart?

No he will never come out because he stay's in my heart.

Talk With God: Thank Jesus for choosing you.

Memory Verse: Hebrews 13:5 (HCSB)- "I will never leave you or forsake you."

Say this verse to someone by memory. Have them initial here when you've done it. _f family_

See if you can say the memory verses from Weeks Eight and Nine without looking.

Week 8: Psalm 122:1(NKJV)- "I was glad when they said to me, 'Let us go into the house of the Lord.'"

Week 9: Mark 16:15 (NKJV)- "And He said to them, 'Go into all the world and preach the gospel to every creature.'"

Am I Different?

Day 1- Phil and Ashley Story

"May I wear my new sneakers?" Ashley asked. "Don't you want to save them for the first day of school?" Mom said.

The sparkly pink sneakers were her prettiest ever. "I'll be careful." She was dying to wear them...and show them off.

"Are you sure? We may be in some rough neighborhoods."

This was the first time Ashley had gone with her parents to feed the homeless. She didn't know what to expect.

First, they went to church where they packaged sandwiches, chips, and cookies. They loaded them into cars already filled with water bottles, toilet paper, socks, toothbrushes, toothpaste, soap, and other things homeless people might need.

The first stop was a used-car dealership. Like

magic, raggedy people appeared from around the side of the building.

Ashley's heart pounded. They looked scary. Some had whiskers. Some wore too many clothes for a hot summer day. Their teeth looked bad. Some smelled.

They gathered around as Dad popped the trunk. Mom handed out meals.

"Thank you," they said.

Ashley helped pass out one meal after another. Dad gave out the other supplies.

Now she felt sorry for them, not scared. Why were they living on the streets? Where were their families? Why couldn't they get a job? She was happy to help them.

When everyone had been fed, they drove to the next stop which was under a highway next to the woods. Homeless people streamed out.

"They live in tents back there," Dad explained.

She spotted a woman and a girl about her age. They wore dirty jeans. They looked messy. Were they homeless too?

The girl headed toward her. Ashley noticed her bare feet. Didn't she have shoes?

"Hi," Ashley said as she handed her a lunch. "Do you need soap or toothpaste or anything?"

The girl looked into the trunk. "Do you have any shoes?"

As Ashley started to say no, she looked down at her sparkly pink sneakers. This girl needed them more than she did.

But could she give them away? She'd wanted to impress her friends.

Did that matter? Maybe what really mattered was not being selfish, being content with her old sneakers, and showing love instead.

She untied her sneakers and handed them to the girl. "Here."

The girl's face lit up. She slipped them on. They fit perfectly.

Her smile made it all worthwhile.

Talk With God: Talk with God about what you learned from this story.

Memory Verse: Matthew 5:16(NKJV)- "Let your light so shine before men, that they may see your good works and glorify your Father in heaven."

Explain in your own words what this verse means.

_____
_____
_____
_____

DAY 2- BE LOVING

If you have asked Jesus into your heart, people should see something different about you. Like what? Read John 13:34-35.

What command does Jesus give?

you Love one another; as I have loved you, that you also love one another.

How will other people know that you are a disciple or follower of Jesus?

they will pay attention to Your personality.

How did Ashley show she loved Jesus?

Ashley and her parents helped the parents

Are you loving to the people around you? It can be hardest to show love to your brothers and sisters or people who are mean to you. Who is someone you find hard to love?

Do something to show love to them this week. Write down what you did and when you did it.

_____

_____

_____

_____

Talk With God: Ask God to forgive you for the times you've been mean and unloving.

Memory Verse: Matthew 5:16(NKJV)- "Let your light so shine before men, that they may see your good works and glorify your Father in heaven."

DAY 3- DON'T WORRY

R ead Philippians 4:6-7.
What do these verses tell you not to do?

_____

_____

_____

_____

What are you supposed to do instead?

_____

_____

_____

_____

What, then, does God promise to give you?

_____

_____

_____

_____

What is something you worry about?

_____

_____

_____

_____

When others see that you don't worry, they will know something is different about you.

Talk With God: Thank God for all He has done for you. Share with Him what you are worried about and ask Him to take care of it.

Memory Verse: Matthew 5:16(NKJV)- "Let your light so shine before men, that they may see your good works and glorify your Father in heaven."

DAY 4- BE HUMBLE

Ashley couldn't wait to show off her new sneakers at school. Why? She wanted to be a little better than everyone else. She wanted to brag. Do you think this would have pleased Jesus? _____

Instead, God wants you to be humble. What does it mean to be humble? It is not thinking about yourself all the time. It is not trying to be better than everyone else. It is treating others better than yourself. This is hard, isn't it? But Jesus is our example. Even though He was God, He humbled Himself by coming to earth and being born in a lowly manger. When He died on the cross, He was not thinking about Himself. He was thinking about you.

Read Philippians 2:3-4(TLB)- "Don't be selfish; don't live to make a good impression on others. Be humble, thinking of others as better than yourself. Don't just think about your own affairs, but be interested in others, too, and in what they are doing."

What does this verse tell you not to do?

_____

_____

_____

_____

What are you supposed to do instead?

_____

_____

_____

What if you can do something better than anyone else? Is it okay to brag then? Why not?

_____

_____

_____

_____

When others see that you aren't selfish and don't brag, they will know something is different about you.

Talk With God: Think of a time when you were selfish, or tried to be better than someone else, or tried to be first, or have the biggest and best. The great news is that God will forgive you and can help you to be humble. Ask God for help to put others first.

Memory Verse: Matthew 5:16(NKJV)- "Let your light so shine before men, that they may see your good works and glorify your Father in heaven."

DAY 5- DON'T COMPLAIN

R ead Philippians 2:14-15.
What do these verses tell you not to do?

_____

_____

_____

_____

What are you supposed to be instead?

_____

_____

_____

_____

God wants you to shine like

_____

_____

_____

_____

When God helps you not to grumble and complain and argue, you will stand out like a shining star in a dark world. Others will know something is different about you.

The next time you start to complain, pray and ask God to help you find something to be thankful for instead.

Talk With God: Ask God to help you shine like a star for His glory. Ask God to forgive you for the times you've grumbled or complained or argued. Think of three things you are thankful for.

Memory Verse: Matthew 5:16(NKJV)- "Let your light so shine before men, that they may see your good works and glorify your Father in heaven."

DAY 6- BE CONTENT

Read Hebrews 13:5(HCSB)-"Your life should be free from the love of money. Be satisfied with what you have, for He Himself has said, 'I will never leave you or forsake you.'"

What are you not to love?

_____

_____

_____

_____

What are you supposed to be instead?

_____

_____

_____

_____

What is the reason given at the end of the verse?

_____

_____

_____

_____

Is there something that you really, really want right now? If so, what?

_____

_____

_____

_____

Is it something you absolutely need?

_____

_____

_____

_____

If it isn't, ask God to help you be content and satisfied even without it.

Talk With God: Thank God that He will never leave you. Thank God for all the good things He has given you. Ask Him to help you be satisfied with what you have.

Memory Verse: Matthew 5:16(NKJV)- "Let your light so shine before men, that they may see your good works and glorify your Father in heaven."

DAY 7- BE A LIGHT

Read Matthew 5:14-16.
You are

_____

_____

_____

_____

Why should you let your light shine?

_____

_____

_____

_____

The reason we are to be different from the world is not so they will think we're so great, but why?

_____

_____

_____

_____

Ashley's light was shining brightly when she gave up her sparkly pink sneakers. Is your light shining? Can people see that you are different? Can people see you love Jesus?

Talk With God: Tell God that you want your life to glorify and praise Him.

Memory Verse: Matthew 5:16(NKJV)- "Let your light so shine before men, that they may see your good works and glorify your Father in heaven."

Say this verse to someone by memory. Have them initial here when you've done it.

_____

_____

_____

_____

See if you can say the memory verses from Weeks Nine and Ten without looking.

Week 9: Mark 16:15 (NKJV)- "And He said to them, 'Go into all the world and preach the gospel to every creature.'"

Week 10: Hebrews 13:5 (HCSB)- "I will never leave you or forsake you."

What Does God Want Me to Be?

Day 1- Phil and Ashley Story

Phil jumped out of bed. He and Matt planned to build a fort in the woods today. He didn't want to waste a minute of this Saturday.

He stepped over the dirty clothes piled on the rug. More were draped over his chair. Library books covered his desk. Stinky socks peeked out from under the bed. Two cups were on his nightstand.

Today was cleaning day. Mom wouldn't let him leave until his room was spotless.

Ugh! Cleaning was his least favorite thing to do. Couldn't he sneak out without Mom knowing?

Maybe, but that wouldn't be right. He needed to obey and get it over with.

He scooped up the dirty clothes and stuffed them into the hamper. He dumped the library books into a backpack. He ran the cups down to the kitchen. He lugged the vacuum cleaner back up.

He vacuumed up every piece of lint. Was he done?

No, his dresser and nightstand were dusty. Would Mom notice? Of course.

He grabbed a dust cloth from the hall closet and skimmed it over the furniture. Now it looked good.

As he took the vacuum cleaner back downstairs, he saw popcorn on the living room rug from their movie last night. Mom needed to clean that up.

Wait a minute. He had the vacuum cleaner in his hands. He should do it.

But it wasn't his job. He didn't *have* to do it.

No, but think what a help it would be to Mom.

In a few minutes, it was cleaned up.

Mom poked her head in. "I don't believe it."

He grinned.

"Oh, honey, thank you." She gave him a big hug.

He felt great. He was glad he had gone above and beyond. With a cheerful attitude, no less.

Not only was Mom pleased, but God was too.

Talk With God: Talk with God about what you learned from this story.

Memory Verse: Ephesians 4:32(NKJV)- "And be kind to one another, tenderhearted, forgiving one another, just as God in Christ also forgave you."

Explain in your own words what this verse means.

_____

_____

_____

_____

DAY 2- OBEDIENT

Read John 14:15.
If you love Jesus, what will you do?

_____

_____

_____

_____

Where do we find God's commandments?

_____

_____

_____

_____

You need to read the Bible to know what God wants you to do. And then you need to obey what God says.

Whom else should you obey? Read Ephesians 6:1.

_____

_____

_____

_____

How did Phil obey his mom?

_____

_____

_____

_____

Can you think of anyone else you should obey and show respect to?

_____

_____

_____

_____

How has choosing to love and obey God helped you this week?

_____

_____

_____

_____

Talk With God: Ask God to show you what He wants you to do and thank Him for helping you to do things which please Him.

Memory Verse: Ephesians 4:32(NKJV)- "And be kind to one another, tenderhearted, forgiving one another, just as God in Christ also forgave you."

DAY 3-FAITHFUL

Read Luke 16:10a (HCSB)- "Whoever is faithful in very little is also faithful in much."

God wants you to be __faithful__.

Faithfulness means you can be counted on to do what you say you will do. When you show you can finish little jobs, then you can be trusted with bigger jobs.

How did Phil show faithfulness?

_____

_____

_____

_____

Can you be counted on to do what you say you will do? __yes , Sometimes__

Think of some little job you finished at home or school or church.

_____

_____

_____

_____

Talk With God: Ask God to help you be faithful and serve Him.

Memory Verse: Ephesians 4:32(NKJV)- "And be kind to one another, tenderhearted, forgiving one another, just as God in Christ also forgave you."

DAY 4-ENTHUSIASTIC

W hat is another way to please God? Read
Colossians 3:23.

How are we to do everything?

_____
_____
_____
_____

What is a job you don't like to do?

_____
_____
_____
_____

Do you sometimes grumble and complain when
you don't want to do something? Do you do it fast and
sloppy just to get it over with? Is that the right way
to behave?

_____
_____
_____
_____

What job didn't Phil like to do?

_____
_____
_____
_____

He did it anyway, and he did a good job. In fact, he did more that he had to.

Jesus watches everything you do. We are to work enthusiastically to please Jesus, not to please our parents or teachers.

Next time you have a job you don't like, do it to please Jesus.

Talk With God: Ask God to forgive you for the times you've grumbled and complained and done a half-hearted job. Ask Him to help you love Him more.

Memory Verse: Ephesians 4:32(NKJV)- "And be kind to one another, tenderhearted, forgiving one another, just as God in Christ also forgave you."

DAY 5-A SERVANT

Jesus doesn't want you to think you're greater and better than everyone else.

Read Mark 10:43-45.

What does Jesus say you must do to be great in God's eyes?

_____

_____

_____

_____

Jesus is our example. Even though he was the God of the universe, He humbled himself and came to earth as a baby and served us by dying for us.

How did Phil serve Mom?

_____

_____

_____

_____

God is pleased when you serve. Think of something you could do this week for someone else.

_____

_____

_____

_____

Talk With God: Ask God to help you love and serve someone this week.

Memory Verse: Ephesians 4:32(NKJV)- "And be kind to one another, tenderhearted, forgiving one another, just as God in Christ also forgave you."

DAY 6- KIND

Read Ephesians 4:32.
What do you think it means to be kind?

_____

_____

_____

_____

Is there anyone you have not been kind to?

_____

_____

_____

_____

What should you do?

_____

_____

_____

_____

Name something kind you will do for someone today or tomorrow.

_____

_____

_____

_____

Talk With God: Ask God to help you to be kind. Ask Him to forgive you for a time you were not kind.

Memory Verse: Ephesians 4:32(NKJV)- "And be kind to one another, tenderhearted, forgiving one another, just as God in Christ also forgave you."

DAY 7- FRIENDLY

Proverbs 18:24(NKJV) says, "A man who has friends must himself be friendly, but there is a friend that sticks closer than a brother."

According to this verse, how does a man have friends?

_____

_____

_____

_____

One of the best ways to show you are a Christian is to be friendly. No one will want to listen to you tell about Jesus if you are not friendly, nice, and kind. An important place to be friendly is in church. No matter how good the teacher is, kids will not want to come back if you are not friendly.

Are you friendly? _y yes_____

Think of someone who needs a friend. Write their name here. _____

Talk With God: Ask God to help you be friendly to that person this week.

Memory Verse: Ephesians 4:32(NKJV)- "And be kind to one another, tenderhearted, forgiving one another, just as God in Christ also forgave you."

Say this verse to someone by memory. Have them initial here when you've done it. _H̶j̶_____

See if you can say the memory verses from Weeks Ten and Eleven without looking.

Week 10: Hebrews 13:5 (HCSB)- "I will never leave you or forsake you."

Week 11: Matthew 5:16(NKJV)- "Let your light so shine before men, that they may see your good works and glorify your Father in heaven."

You did it! You finished!

I hope you know God better now. The more time you spend with Him, the closer you will feel to Him.

So, don't stop now. Even though this book is finished, don't stop having a Quiet Time every day.

- Read a few verses in the Bible. Read it as if it were a letter from God just to you.
- Think about what you have read and how it applies to you.
- Praise and worship God
- Confess your sins
- Pray for yourself and others

My prayer for you is that you will love God with all your heart and follow Him all the days of your life.

Beth Livingston

MEMORY VERSES

Week 1- Am I a Christian?
John 3:16 (NIV)- "For God so loved the world that he gave his one and only Son, that whoever believes in him shall not perish but have eternal life."

Week 2- What Happened When I Became a Christian?
2 Corinthians 5:17 (NKJV)- "Therefore, if anyone is in Christ, he is a new creation; old things have passed away; behold, all things have become new."

Week 3- Who is God?
I Chronicles 29:11(NIV)- "Yours, O Lord, is the greatness and the power and the glory and the majesty and the splendor, for everything in heaven and earth is yours."

Week 4- Who is Jesus?
Hebrews 9:22 (NIV)- "...without the shedding of blood there is no forgiveness."

Week 5- Who is the Holy Spirit?
Galatians 5:22-23(NIV)- "But the fruit of the Spirit is love, joy, peace, patience, kindness, goodness, faithfulness, gentleness, and self-control..."

Week 6- Why is the Bible So Important?

1 Peter 2:2(NKJV)- "As newborn babes, desire the pure milk of the word that you may grow thereby."

Week 7- Why Pray?

Matthew 21:22 (NIV)- "And all things, whatever you ask in prayer, believing, you will receive."

Week 8- Why Go to Church?

Psalm 122:1(NKJV)- "I was glad when they said to me, 'Let us go into the house of the Lord.'"

Week 9- How Do I Tell Others About Jesus?

Mark 16:15 (NKJV)- "And He said to them, 'Go into all the world and preach the gospel to every creature.'"

Week 10- If I Sin, Will Jesus Come Out of My Heart?

Hebrews 13:5 (HCSB)- "I will never leave you or forsake you."

Week 11- Am I Different?

Matthew 5:16(NKJV)- "Let your light so shine before men, that they may see your good works and glorify your Father in heaven."

Week 12- What Does God Want Me to Be?

Ephesians 4:32(NKJV)- "And be kind to one another, tenderhearted, forgiving one another, just as God in Christ also forgave you."

ACKNOWLEDGMENTS

When I was twelve years old, my father, Irving O. Larson, wrote *Basics for Believers*, a discipleship workbook for new believers. After he died in 2013, as I revised and updated it, I recognized the need to have such a book for children. I used many of his ideas in developing this book. Thanks, Dad.

My brother, David Larson, wrote a *Disciple Bible Study Course* to use with his ministry to international students. I also borrowed ideas from him. Thanks for sharing, David.

Many thanks to the following people who proofread my manuscript and gave such helpful suggestions:

David Livingston   Eleanor Larson
Pastor Shannon Hollinger   Megan Hess
Pastor Rob Barlow   Tina Benedict
Margaret Mokry   Bev Caldwell
                                Carol Oakley

And thanks to my team of young readers who did

this as a Bible study together with their moms, Laura Gardner and Kristen Baker.

Brooke Gardner   Lexi Baker
Jacob Gardner   Sophia Baker

To God be the glory.

ABOUT THE AUTHOR

Beth Livingston loves Jesus and loves to tell kids about Jesus. A former school librarian, she is now retired and lives with her husband in Dublin, Ohio, where she spends her days writing.

She is pictured here with her grandchildren, Brooke and Jacob, who were the first kids, along with their friends Lexi and Sophia, to do *Basics for Believing Kids*.

Beth has also written two fiction books for kids:

The Hideout
Susanna of Beaver Lodge

and five Christian Historical novels for adults:

Tour of Mansions series-

*The Chautauqua Belles,
The Easterly House,* and
Sunnyside Hill

Tour of Homes series-

The Kenton House and *Mount Olive*

Website: http://bethlivingston.net/
Facebook: https://www.facebook.com/
authorbethlivingston
Email: authorbethlivingston@gmail.com
Beth's Bible Stories for Kids Blog: http://blog.
bethlivingston.net/

Made in the USA
Coppell, TX
26 February 2024

29453114R00095